JESSE OWENS

SPORTS UNITE US

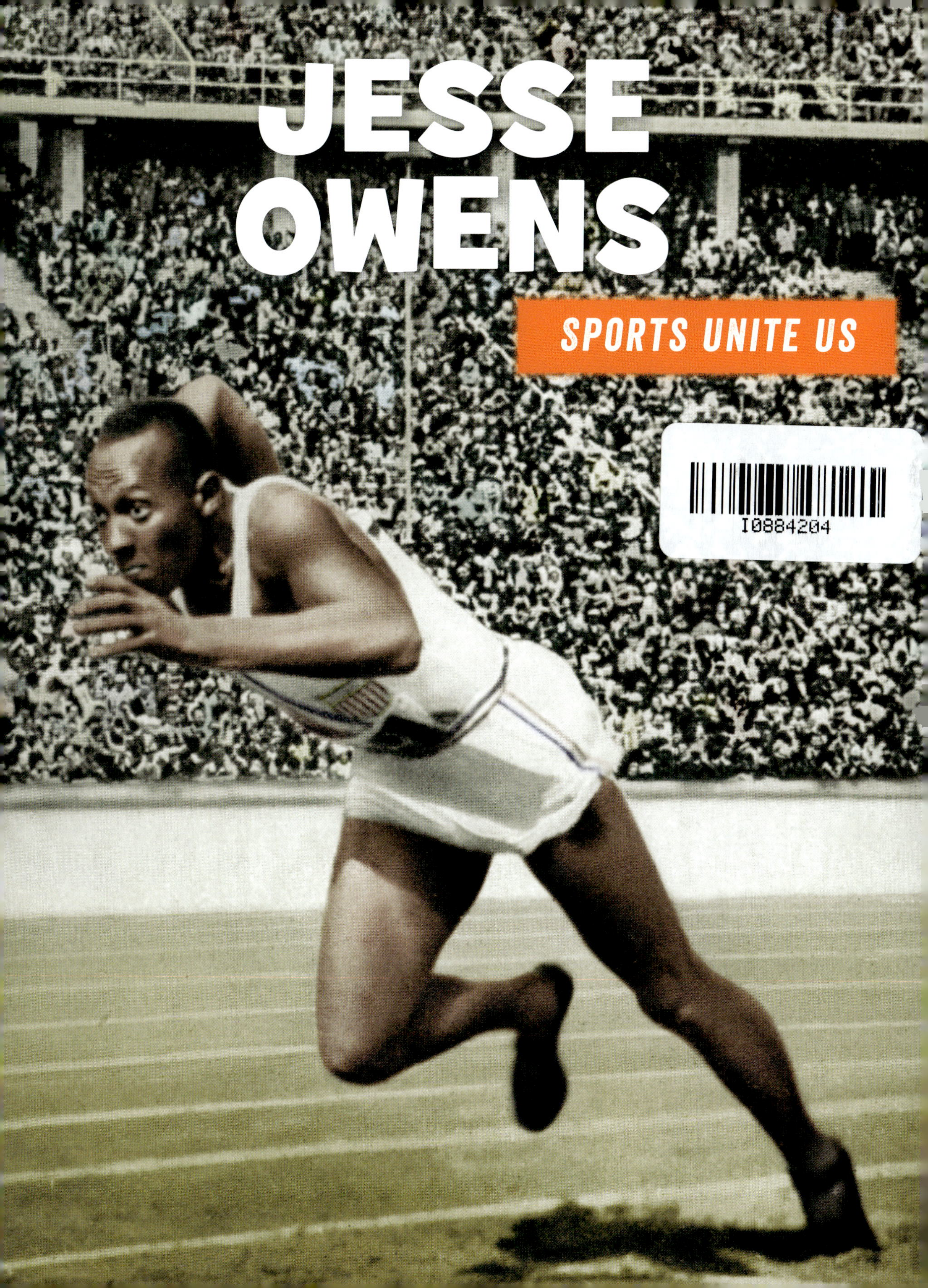

Published in the United States of America by Cherry Lake Publishing
Ann Arbor, Michigan
www.cherrylakepublishing.com

Reading Adviser: Marla Conn MS, Ed., Literacy specialist, Read-Ability, Inc.

Photo Credits: ©Getty Images, cover; ©The Print Collector / Heritage-Images/Newscom, 1; ©Everett Collection/Newscom, 5; ©UPPA/Photoshot/Newscom, 6; ©Keystone/Getty Images, 9; ©Akg-images/Newscom, 10; ©TALKING SPORT/Photoshot/Newscom, 13; ©TALKING SPORT/Photoshot/Newscom, 14; ©Photoshot/Newscom, 16; ©picture-alliance/Newscom, 19; ©Michael Steele/Getty Images, 20; ©Everett Collection/Newscom, 23; ©U.S. National Archives and Records Administration/Wikimedia, 25; ©Angelo Cozzi/Wikimedia, 26; ©UPPA/Photoshot/Newscom, 28; ©Neftali/Shutterstock, 28; ©/Getty Images, 29; ©UPI/Newscom, 29; ©picture-alliance/Newscom, 30

Library of Congress Cataloging-in-Publication Data has been filed and is available at catalog.loc.gov

Cherry Lake Publishing would like to acknowledge the work of The Partnership for 21st Century Learning.
Please visit *www.p21.org* for more information.

Printed in the United States of America
Corporate Graphics

ABOUT THE AUTHOR

Heather Williams is a writer and educator with a passion for seeing readers of all ages connect with others through stories and personal experiences. She enjoys running, reading, and watching sports. Heather lives in Greensboro, North Carolina with her husband and two children.

TABLE OF CONTENTS

Jim Crow and Adolf Hitler

The **ancient** Olympic Games began in 776 BCE. For hundreds of years, many of the main events were track and field sports. **Sprints**, long jumps, and the **marathon** are examples of track and field sports. Track and field competitions like those at the ancient Olympics are still part of the **modern** games. Today, we gather around our televisions and computers to watch the Olympics. Track stars, such as Usain Bolt and Mo Farah, amaze us with record-breaking speed. But more than 75 years ago, a man named Jesse Owens ran the races of his life at the 1936 Olympics.

The 1930s were a time of difficulty for American people. The **Great Depression** had left most Americans poor and jobless. Severe **drought** made farming almost impossible. Many banks

Jobless Americans were forced to stand in line for basic items like bread and milk during the Great Depression.

closed, and some people lost what little money they had. Americans had to stand in free-food lines to feed their families. President Franklin D. Roosevelt promised to help Americans recover with his New Deal programs. He planned to create many new jobs.

Life was even more challenging for African Americans. **Segregation** and **racism** limited their rights and made it hard for them to get jobs. Local and state laws known as "Jim Crow" laws meant that black Americans had separate schools, bathrooms, and even water fountains. Business owners did not

Adolf Hitler oversaw the opening of the 1936 Summer Olympic Games in Berlin, Germany.

have to hire African Americans, according to Jim Crow laws. Hotels and restaurants could refuse to serve black people. White Americans **discriminated** against black Americans and often mistreated them.

Across the ocean in Germany lived a man named Adolf Hitler. Hitler was the leader of the **Nazi Party**. He was also practicing discrimination. Hitler believed that white people were better than all other races. He especially disliked black and Jewish people. The German government closed black- and Jewish-owned businesses. They were also not allowed to use public trains and buses. Jews and blacks could only go to certain stores and live in certain neighborhoods. Many blacks and Jews left Germany during this time.

The 1936 Olympics were held in Berlin, Germany. Runners carried the Olympic torch from Greece to the opening ceremony of the Olympics for the first time. The 1936 Olympics were also the first to be shown on television. Germans thought of sports as a way to show strength and power. Hitler wanted the Olympic Games to prove that the white race was better, stronger, and faster than other races. Hitler was not prepared for the speed of Jesse Owens.

Plessy v. Ferguson

Jim Crow laws were only enforced in certain states at first. In 1892, a man who was part African American refused to get off of an all-white train car in Louisiana. His name was Homer Plessy. He was arrested and his case went to the Supreme Court of the United States. The Supreme Court decided that it was legal for a state to make black people use separate facilities. After Plessy v. Ferguson, "separate but equal" laws began to be enforced across the country.

The Buckeye Bullet

Jesse Owens was born in Oakville, Alabama, in 1913. He was the youngest of 10 children. Jesse's family moved to Cleveland, Ohio, in search of a better life when he was 9. His full name was James Cleveland Owens. He went by the nickname J.C. When he told his new teacher his name, she misunderstood his southern accent. She thought he said "Jesse." The name stuck for the rest of his life.

Jesse's junior high track coach noticed that he had a gift for running. The coach encouraged him to compete. Jesse had a job after school, so his coach let him practice before school. Jesse's coach was his first role model. He was a white man who saw Jesse as a talented athlete. He showed Jesse that it was possible for white and black people to be friends.

Jesse Owens, left, and Ralph Metcalfe were among 18 African American athletes who competed in the 1936 Summer Olympics.

When Jesse was in high school, he ran the 100-yard dash in the world-record time of 9.4 seconds. He competed at the 1933 National Interscholastic Track and Field Championship in Chicago. After high school, many colleges and universities tried to **recruit** Jesse. He chose to attend Ohio State University so he could be close to his family.

There were no athletic **scholarships** for African American students in the 1930s. Ohio State was a segregated college, and very few black students went there. It was known for discrimination against African Americans. Jesse hoped to make a

Jesse Owens broke or tied four world records in 45 minutes at the Big Ten Track and Field Championships in 1935.

difference at Ohio State by working hard and doing his best. He worked hard to pay for his school fees. Jesse's running ability was well known at Ohio State. He became captain of the track and field team. Jesse was known as the Buckeye Bullet.

In 1935, Jesse and the Ohio State track and field team went to the Big Ten Track and Field Championships in Michigan. The night before the meet, Jesse fell down some stairs and hurt his back. His team was afraid he would not be able to run. But Jesse got treatment for his back and competed anyway. He won four events that day: the 100-yard dash, the long jump, the 220-yard dash, and the 220-yard hurdles. In 45 minutes, Jesse set three world records and tied another world record.

Jesse's success at Ohio State made him very popular. He was admired by both white and black fans. The African American community saw him as a hero for becoming a track star at a segregated college. At national track meets in California and Nebraska, fans stood in line for Jesse's autograph. He met famous actors, such as Will Rogers and Mae West. In 1936, he went to the Olympic trials in New York. The Buckeye Bullet was heading for the 1936 Olympics in Berlin, Germany.

Athletic Scholarships

An athletic scholarship is an amount of money given to a student for playing a sport at a college or university. Coaches decide which students get scholarships to play on their teams. Scholarships are usually given to students who are very talented in their sport. Only about two percent of high school students are given sports scholarships. When Jesse was in high school, black students were often overlooked for athletic scholarships. Today, students of all races who meet scholarship requirements are **eligible**.

Going for Gold

Before the Olympic team left for Germany, they were treated to many celebrations. The American people were especially excited about what Jesse Owens would achieve at the Olympics. At a special dinner honoring the athletes, Jesse met Babe Ruth. Ruth was a famous baseball player who played for the New York Yankees. He had dinner with Jesse before the Olympics. Ruth told Jesse he wanted to see him win in Berlin.

The U.S. Olympic team sailed to Germany on the SS *Manhattan*. The trip took nine days. There were 334 athletes on board. On the last day of the trip, the athletes picked team **superlatives**. Jesse was voted best-dressed. He was also named the second-most popular athlete on the ship. Jesse enjoyed

Fans flocked to Berlin's Olympic Stadium to watch Jesse Owens compete in the 1936 Olympics.

getting to know his teammates. He also looked forward to meeting athletes from other countries. Jesse believed in the idea that the Olympics were meant to encourage friendship and **unity**. He also wanted to show Hitler and the world that anyone could be a good athlete.

When the team arrived in Berlin, Jesse heard German fans chanting his name. His fame had spread across the world. People gathered around him to get his autograph. Some of his track shoes were even stolen as **souvenirs**. A German filmmaker took

Jesse Owens and his competitors take off from the starting line at the 1936 Summer Olympics.

photos and videos of the Olympics for a movie she was making. She focused more on Jesse than any other athlete at the Olympics. Fans crowded into the Olympic Stadium to see Jesse compete. He did not disappoint them.

Jesse competed in four events in the Berlin Olympics. His first event was the 100-meter sprint. Jesse won that event and earned his first gold medal. His second event was the long jump. A German athlete named Carl Ludwig "Luz" Long noticed Jesse was having some trouble in the **qualifying round**. Long gave

Adidas

When Jesse Owens ran in the 1936 Olympics, he was the first black man to **endorse** a pair of track shoes. The shoes were made by a German company called Gebrüder Dassler Schuhfabrik, or the Dassler Brothers Shoe Factory. Two brothers named Adolf "Adi" and Rudolf "Rudi" Dassler owned the company in Herzogenaurach, Germany. Adi was a sports fan who loved designing shoes. Rudi was an outgoing salesman. In the 1940s, the two had a disagreement. Rudi left the company and started his own shoe business across the river. Adi continued to run the other business. Adi called his company Adidas, and Rudi named his Puma. The two were fierce rivals for many years. The two companies competed for business from sports teams and athletes. Thirty years after the two brothers died, the two companies decided to put aside the family feud. They celebrated with a friendly soccer game.

Jesse Owens (top right) beat teammate Ralph Metcalfe in the 100-meter sprint by a tenth of a second.

him some advice, and Jesse ended up winning the gold medal for the long jump. Jesse also won the gold medal for the 200-meter sprint and the 4x100-meter relay. He was the first American athlete to win four gold medals in the Olympics. Jesse held the record for most gold medals won in the Olympics until 1984.

Adolf Hitler did not congratulate all the athletes for winning medals at the Olympics. At first, he only shook hands with Germans and a few others. The Olympic committee told him he had to congratulate all the athletes or none of them. Hitler chose not to shake hands with any of the athletes. Many people criticized Hitler for this. But Jesse said it was not **sportsmanlike** to criticize the leader of a country you were visiting. Jesse felt that it was more important to focus on the American athletes' accomplishments. The United States won 56 medals in the 1936 Olympics.

The Modern Olympics

The modern Olympic Games began in 1896. Athens, Greece, hosted the first modern Olympics. The Olympics have been held every four years since then. There were 241 athletes from 14 countries at the first modern Olympics. An American track and field athlete named James Connolly was the first Olympic champion. He won a silver medal for the triple jump. Gold medals were not awarded until the 1904 Olympics. Until 1992, the Winter and Summer Olympic Games were held in the same year.

An Unlikely Friendship

Jesse Owens won four gold medals at the Berlin Olympics. But he often said the greatest prize he won that summer was his friendship with Luz Long. Long was a popular athlete in Germany. He was the world-record holder for the long jump. Everyone expected him to win a gold medal at the 1936 Olympics. During the qualifying round for the event, Jesse **fouled** twice. His third jump had to be just right so he could compete in the final event. Jesse often told the story of how Long ran over to talk with him. He claimed that Long gave him advice that helped him make it to the medal round. Jesse ended up beating Long and winning the gold medal for the long jump.

During the medal ceremony for the long jump, Long hugged Jesse. Not only was Long a white man, he was also a German

Owens considered German competitor Luz Long one of the best friends of his lifetime.

citizen under Hitler's rule. Hitler believed white German people were better than all other people. But Long respected Jesse and saw him as an equal. Both men were superior athletes. They were the same age, and both had young children at home. They found a way to talk and get to know each other, even though they spoke different languages. The two friends kept in touch through letters after the Olympics.

Long died in 1943. He was killed while fighting for Germany in World War II (1939–1945). In his last letter to Jesse, he asked

American runner Leonel Manzano wore a Team USA track uniform with Jesse Owens's initials on the shoulder at the 2009 International Association of Athletic Federations track and field competition in Berlin.

his friend to find his son Kai someday. Jesse returned to Berlin in 1951 on a U.S. Department of State tour. There, he met Kai Long. Jesse and Kai began to write letters to each other. Jesse told Kai about his father's kindness and friendship. They kept in touch until Jesse died in 1980.

In 2009, a world track and field competition was held at the Olympic Stadium in Berlin. The U.S. track and field team wore special uniforms with "J.O." on them to honor Jesse. Jesse's granddaughter Marlene attended the competition. Kai was there also. Together, the two of them awarded the medals for the long jump event. They symbolized the friendship that had grown out of the Olympic long jump event more than 70 years earlier. Long and Jesse had shown the world that race did not have to divide people. A love for their sport created a bond that lasted for generations.

The Long Jump

The long jump is one of the oldest Olympic sports. A long jumper starts by running down a short track. When the jumper reaches a take-off board, they jump as far as possible into a sand pit. The jump is measured from the mark in the sand closest to the board. Jesse Owens set the world record for the long jump in 1935. He jumped 8.13 meters. Another American athlete named Bob Beamon broke his record in 1960. Beamon's record of 8.90 meters was broken in 1991. The current long jump record is 8.95 meters.

Walk and Talk

America celebrated Jesse Owens when he returned home from the Olympics. In New York, there was a **ticker tape parade** held in his honor. There was a **reception** for him at the Waldorf Astoria hotel in Manhattan. He was welcomed in Cleveland as a hero. People all around the world knew his name.

Jesse had a number of jobs after the Olympics. He ran a dry-cleaning business, worked as the assistant trainer for the Ohio State track team, and made motivational speeches. Sometimes he ran against horses at baseball games to make extra money.

His biggest passion was helping young people. Jesse had always wanted to be a teacher. During World War II, the U.S. Office of Civilian Defense appointed Jesse as the leader of a national fitness program. His job was to help young African

After the Olympics, Jesse Owens was an advocate for African American youth and encouraged them to participate in sports.

Americans get into good physical and mental shape in case they were called to war. Jesse also worked for the Illinois Youth Commission and directed the South Side Boys Club in Chicago. He saw sports as a way for African American youth to find their place in society.

President Dwight D. Eisenhower appointed Jesse as a U.S. Ambassador of Sports after World War II. Jesse traveled to the Olympics in Australia to represent the president. Jesse also went on a tour of Malaysia, India, and the Philippines. He spoke about friendship between the countries and the United States. He also held running **clinics** for kids he met in other countries. Jesse worked to make the world a better place by helping young people. He believed in hard work and loyalty to America.

The African American community looked to Jesse during the **Civil Rights** Movement in the 1960s. Jesse considered Martin Luther King Jr. a hero. But Jesse did not always agree with protests during the Civil Rights Movement. He thought protests only caused more conflict. Jesse preferred to bring change by setting an example with his own life. He valued relationships with people of all races. Jesse felt friendships were more important than protests. He liked to "walk and talk" with others and learn from them.

Civil Rights Movement

The Civil Rights Movement took place in the 1960s. It was a time when African Americans fought for equal rights in the U.S. There were many important non-violent protests during the Civil Rights Movement. Rosa Parks protested transportation laws by refusing to sit at the back of a bus. Four college students in North Carolina sat at an all-white lunch counter and refused to leave. More than 200,000 people gathered for the March on Washington in 1963. The Civil Rights Act of 1964 gave equal rights to all people of the United States.

Jesse Owens looked up to Martin Luther King Jr., though they did not always agree on how to encourage social change.

Four World Records in 45 Minutes

Jesse Owens matched or set four world records in only 45 minutes at the 1935 Big Ten track meet.

Event	Previous Record	Jesse Owens	Current
100-yard sprint	9.4 seconds	9.4 seconds	9.07 seconds
Long Jump	7.98 meters	8.13 meters	8.95 meters
220-yard sprint*	20.6 seconds	20.3 seconds	19.19 seconds
220-low hurdle**	23 seconds	22.6 seconds	21.9 seconds

**now the 200-meter sprint*

***now the 200-meter hurdles*

Jesse Owens paved the way for other African American athletes at the Olympic Games.

At the 1968 Olympics, two African American athletes planned a protest at the games. Jesse spoke out against using the Olympics for politics. Even though he understood their reasons, Jesse believed the Olympics were supposed to unite people. His own Olympic experience had taken place during a time when racial differences caused conflicts around the world. But he had risen above those conflicts. He had made a lifelong friend and become a celebrated gold medalist. Jesse had never forgotten the power of coming together to compete.

The Legacy of Jesse Owens

Jesse Owens was inducted into the Alabama Sports Hall of Fame in 1970. President Gerald Ford awarded Jesse the Presidential Medal of Freedom in 1976. It is the highest honor an American citizen can receive. After Jesse's death, his wife accepted the Congressional Gold Medal in his honor. Jesse was named the sixth-greatest athlete of the 20th century. USA Track & Field's best athlete award is named after him. In 1984, the city of West Berlin named a street after Jesse. Jesse-Owens-Allee is just outside the Olympic Stadium where Jesse made history. The Jesse Owens Foundation carries out Jesse's devotion to young people by providing scholarships at Ohio State University. President Jimmy Carter said that Jesse's athletic accomplishments and dedication to helping young people made him one of the most important people in American history.

1933

Jesse graduates from East Technical High School and enrolls at Ohio State University, where he is nicknamed the Buckeye Bullet.

1913

Jesse Owens is born in Oakville, Alabama.

1910

1930

1935

Jesse ties one world record and breaks three others at the Big Ten track championship.

1951

Jesse returns to Berlin, where he meets the son of his lifelong friend Luz Long.

1936

Jesse competes in the 1936 Olympics in Berlin, where he becomes the first American athlete to win four gold medals.

1950

1970

1970

Jesse becomes one of the first athletes to be inducted into the Alabama Sports Hall of Fame.

Think About It

Owens and Long overcame many obstacles at the Olympics and in society in general to become lifelong friends. What obstacles do you think they overcame at the Olympics? In society?

There are many stories of unlikely friendships growing from difficult moments in sporting events and competitions like the Olympics. Can you find another example of a friendship similar to Jesse Owens and Luz Long's friendship?

Learn More

BOOKS

Aaseng, Nathan. *Track and Field.* San Diego: Lucent Books, 2002.

Calkhoven, Laurie. *Jesse Owens.* New York: Simon Spotlight, 2017.

Israel, Elaine. *Jesse Owens: Running into History.* New York: Harper Collins, 2008.

ON THE WEB

Civil Rights for Kids
www.ducksters.com/history/civil_rights/jim_crow_laws.php

Jesse Owens, Olympic Legend
www.jesseowens.com

The Olympic Games
www.olympic.org/Jesse-Owens

GLOSSARY

ancient (AYN-shunt) something from the very distant past that no longer exists

civil rights (SI-vel RITES) political and social freedom and equality

clinics (KLI-niks) gatherings where coaching in a sport is given to small groups

discriminate (diss-CREM-uh-nayt) to treat someone badly because of race

drought (DROWT) a lack of rain that makes it very hard to grow crops

eligible (ELL-uh-jib-ull) having the necessary requirements

endorse (in-dorss) in sports, when a well known athlete wears a brand of shoe or clothing

foul (FOWL) in the long jump, when the jumper steps past the board

Great Depression (grayt duh-PRESH-unn) a time during the 1930s when many people were out of work, lost their homes, and went hungry due to a lack of money

marathon (MARE-uh-thon) a 26.2 mile run

modern (MAH-durn) something happening in the present time

Nazi Party (NOT-zee PAR-tee) a political group that ruled Germany from 1933-1945

qualifying round (KWA-lih-fy-eeng ROUND) in the Olympics, the match or event that must be won to get to the medal round

racism (RAY-siz-uhm) belief that one race is better than another

reception (REE-sep-shun) a small party in someone's honor

recruit (ree-KROOT) when a college or university coach tries to get an athlete to join a sports team

scholarships (SKAH-lur-ships) money given to students to pay for college

segregation (seg-gruh-GAY-shun) system of setting one race apart from another

souvenirs (soo-vuh-NEERS) objects kept as a reminder of a person, place, or event

sportsmanlike (SPORTS-mun-like) acting in a friendly way, especially toward an opposing team or player

sprints (SPRENTS) very fast runs over short distances

superlatives (soo-PUR-lah-tivs) highest praise in particular areas

ticker tape parade (TIK-urr-tayp puh-RAYD) a parade usually held in a large city where large amounts of confetti are thrown in celebration

unity (YOO-nuh-tee) coming together

INDEX